The Millionaire Mindset Shift

Renew Your Thoughts, Redefine Your Wealth

By: Yvette Lloyd

Dedicated to Sherice Thompson

July 1958 – October 2019

A woman whose hands built streets,

but whose heart built legacies.

Your strength paved the foundation of my life.

Your wisdom shaped my mind.

Your sacrifices created my purpose.

Your love taught me how to become everything you dreamed of.

I am because you were.

And everything I build will carry your name.

I love you forever, Mom.

Table of Contents

Introduction

I created this book to offer an honest and real look at the **highs and lows of entrepreneurship**. While I've heard countless success stories, many don't delve deeply into the struggles or how individuals rebuilt from their lowest points. My goal is to be completely transparent with my own journey.

I want to inspire you to **keep going** even when the path feels impossible and your dreams seem out of reach. It's okay not to succeed on the first, second, or even third try. What truly matters is learning from your mistakes and **persevering**.

I'm genuinely tired of the "I got rich overnight!" narratives and "get rich quick" scams. The stories that truly motivate me are those of resilience - how success took multiple attempts and years of dedication. I hope this book offers you that same kind of motivation, encouraging you to push forward through failed businesses, the loss of friends, financial setbacks, and even heartache.

Entrepreneurship isn't for the faint of heart, but it is, without a doubt, **well worth it**.

Chapter 1

Entrepreneurship

Entrepreneurship has always been in my blood, even as a child. At the young age of eight, we lived in a close-knit community. I always felt that I was a leader in many ways, even at that age. I consistently took the leadership role when it came to myself and the children who lived in my community. I remember when my mom used to go to the grocery store or run errands, I would gather all the children in the community, line them up, and make sandwiches for them. I always had a giving spirit. I loved taking care of people, which I considered a gift and a curse.

I know my mom used to be upset that I used her hard-earned money and groceries to feed the children in the community. It got to the point where my mom started putting money aside to help me with my goal of feeding my community.

When I was in 4th or 5th grade, my stepfather made me read and then write an essay about what I'd just read. More than anything, he wanted me to develop **comprehension skills**. As a kid, I was furious about having to read during summer breaks. All I wanted to do was play outside with my friends. Looking back now, though, I clearly see the value in what he was doing and the person he was pushing me to become.

My mother's relationship with reading was unique. She knew how to read, but in some instances, she struggled. She had a special way of understanding text. To this day, I struggle with reading, much like her. However, I was able to comprehend, and both my mom and stepfather felt that was important.

I was truly motivated by my stepfather. Watching him become an entrepreneur ignited something within me. He started by buying the property next door, which opened his gateway into the real estate business. He expanded, acquiring apartments, commercial buildings, and houses. To supplement his income, he also cut grass and eventually started a **lawn care business**, even though they weren't popular back then. I watched him build his business from the ground up.

At a young age, I wanted to learn more about business and make my own money, just like him. However, my mom wouldn't let me get a job in high school. She wanted me to focus on school and sports, then worry about a job later in life. But all I wanted to be was a **BOSS**!

NOTES

Chapter 2

Becoming A Boss

At the age of 17, I graduated from high school and decided to give college a try, as it felt like the expected next step. I was the first person in my family to attend college. My first year at Kent State University, I received all F's. I wasn't passionate about college, and I didn't think it was for me, but I was pursuing a nursing degree because I knew it was a necessary step to become a brain surgeon.

While in school, I also took free EMT classes at the hospital where my grandmother worked. I was set on being an EMT until one day I experienced a series of events that made me rethink my calling. First, a patient with HIV threatened to pull her IV out of her arm, and it scared me. Then, a man who had been shot tried to flirt with me while he was bleeding. Later, we had a patient who was around 500 pounds and wanted us to carry her down the stairs. After dealing with all of that in a single day, I realized that being an EMT was not my calling.

After realizing that being an EMT wasn't for me, my nephew was born, and I decided to get a job at his daycare. I started in the infant room and worked my way up, moving to the toddler room and then to the pre-school room. I even worked in the kitchen, cooking for the kids, before I was promoted to the office.

While working in the office, I began to learn the business side of things. This, along with my hands-on experience in each classroom and the kitchen, prepared me to start my own daycare. It was a natural fit for me, as I'd always loved children and had a giving spirit, just like when I used to feed the kids in my old community.

At this time, I was in my last year of college and changed my major from nursing to **Early Childhood Education**. This new major, combined with my personal experience at the daycare, put me on the right path to learning the ropes of the business.

Please note that this wasn't an overnight success. I worked at that daycare for years before starting my own business. I wanted to learn all I could and gain the necessary experience to run a successful daycare.

Before I officially started my daycare, a parent from the daycare where I was working reached out to me. She worked for a huge car retail company and asked if I would watch her child privately at my home. She even offered to pay me the same weekly rate she was paying at the daycare. I didn't know what the daycare was charging, so I looked it up, and my interest was immediately piqued.

So, while still working at the daycare, I started babysitting in my home. I even took a babysitting course because I wanted to be as prepared as possible. Soon, I was getting calls from other parents who worked the second shift at the same car retail company and needed childcare.

I was making good money and truly enjoyed what I was doing. I would braid the children's hair and simply love on them. I was an extreme hustler and had several streams of income at that time.

Unfortunately, I was in a bad relationship, so I decided to break up with him and move back into my own home. This turned out to be a blessing in disguise because I decided to turn my house into a daycare. With no mentor or assistance, I had to do all the research on my own to figure out what I needed to start an in-home daycare.

I learned how to start a **Type B childcare home**, which allowed me to care for up to six children, with a maximum of three being under the age of two. Type B providers also have to be licensed.

At the same time, I started my youth program, which began with just a few girls. I didn't receive any funding or assistance from the state or the girls' parents. I funded the program entirely with the money I earned from my daycare. I would buy the girls food, clothes, supplies, or whatever they needed. My youth program met once a week at my home.

When I first started my in-home daycare, you might have thought I was making good money, but that wasn't the case. My car was repossessed because I wasn't earning enough, partly because I was using the daycare's money to fund my youth program. I saw the vision, but my funds didn't match my ambition at the time.

My mom and aunt helped me as much as they could, and I was still receiving government assistance like food stamps and Medicaid. Having only three to four kids enrolled in my daycare didn't cover my bills, but I kept working and had the support of my aunt and mother until I got back on my feet. Then, I learned about **Type A childcare**.

Type A childcare is a licensed program where I could care for up to 12 children in my home. My home had to meet specific licensing requirements, and for it to be approved as a Type A program, I had to meet with the city council to be voted in and have my home approved as a commercial property.

Thankfully, I was related to half the people on my street because I also had to get my neighbors' approval. Once I received that approval, the money started to flow. I was making at least $6,000 to $8,000 a week, and my enrollment quickly filled up. Things were finally going well for me, but I wish I had some financial structure.

NOTES

Chapter 3

Financial Structure

Many new entrepreneurs think that getting an LLC and an EIN is all it takes to be in business. I certainly did. But I quickly learned that there's so much more to it. As a business owner, you have to remember to **renew with the state each year**, pay federal and state income taxes, and cover city and state self-employment taxes. If you have employees, you also have to report to unemployment and pay payroll taxes.

When I started, I had no idea what the hell I was doing. My lack of knowledge combined with my inability to set boundaries with people put me $60,000 in debt. It's hard to pay these necessary fees and taxes when you're already in a financial hole. Learning these lessons the hard way was tough, but it taught me the importance of being fully informed before you dive in.

I don't regret my choices, but I do wish I had **financial structure**. I wish I had an accountant to help me manage my money instead of pouring it all back into my community. I was doing everything for everybody, paying for my youth group girls' hair and clothes, feeding them, and even helping their parents with utility bills. I was constantly spending without organizing my money or prioritizing my own needs. I funded friends' businesses and paid for personal trips, all while pouring into others with no one pouring back into me. In the long run, that really hurt me.

People can take advantage of your generosity when they notice you're making money and have a kind heart. That's exactly what happened to me. I was constantly spending, and everyone around me just kept taking. It was never enough; they always wanted more.

The same people I helped were often the first to turn on me if I made a mistake or simply said "no." They offered no grace and treated me terribly, even though I knew they'd been through worse with other people. In my youth group, the girls all had different needs, and some clung to me more than others. This led to accusations of favoritism. I had no boundaries with people I considered friends, mentees, and even their parents. They were always in my home, watching my every move. They saw so much of my life that they started creating their own theories about how I made my money. Since I never showed my struggles, all they saw was the financial outcome. They had no idea I was in a bad place financially because I was spending so much on them.

I even hired some parents to work for me so they could keep the benefits they were receiving, paying them half in cash and half by check. But even that wasn't enough. I took in one girl from the streets to keep her safe, and she ended up hurting me the most. After giving someone food, clothing, and a place to live, being betrayed by them was incredibly painful. All of this goes back to my lack of boundaries.

When I started my business, people saw the success but not the struggle. The sense of entitlement my friends had was unbelievable. They got mad if I did anything for myself. When they started their own businesses similar to mine, they treated it like a competition. But I was never competing with anyone. This was the mission God gave me, and I stayed in my own lane.

These experiences taught me several lessons. I should have set **boundaries** and limited my conversations with others instead of telling them everything and letting them watch my every move. I was sharing too much, and some things like my plans should have been kept to myself. I also learned that people I considered friends would gang up on me, even if they hated each other. Unfortunately, these events put me in a really dark place. I went through so much alone, and no one knew what I was going through.

I was always genuine in my work. I did so much in the community that I often had community leaders, city council members, and politicians come by for photo ops, but none of them ever helped me get **funding**. I was completely on my own. I did manage to enroll in one program that gave me $500 a month for my business. I later found out they used my data to secure over a million dollars in funding and grants for themselves. As soon as they got their money, they let me go. It was heartbreaking to be used like that and then dumped. I guess that's politics for you.

To make things worse, because I worked with inner-city children, my youth program was kicked out of several buildings. They would create false narratives about the kids to get us removed. The city council members and community leaders all assumed I was receiving thousands of dollars in funding, but I wasn't. I just made the shit look good. I was using my own money to fund everything for my youth program—from field trips to van rentals and hotel stays. Some parents weren't helping or participating; it was all on me.

Nine years ago, I reached my breaking point after going through several locations. The building was depressing—it looked like a prison. But I saw potential, so I started decorating and giving it life with my own creative spin.

Before I came, there were no kids. I single-handedly brought in an abundance of children, which led to the building receiving more funding. And, of course, they never gave me a dime. The entire time I was there, they only took from me. Despite all the money I poured into the building and the number of kids I brought in, they never helped me get grants or funding.

I started organizing community events like lock-ins for the girls and boys, inviting community leaders to come speak to them. Some spoke for free, while others charged me. I also hosted events for breast cancer and domestic violence survivors. I even paid for a publicist every month to help promote my business which was located inside of their building, which benefited them as well. For these events, I paid for everything myself—food, drinks, decorations, and even some of the girls' formal dresses.

In addition to hosting events, I created the **Young Boss Expo**, an entrepreneurship event for kids ages 4 to 18. I had my youth group girls help plan it to teach them leadership skills. Some of the girls even wanted to become publicists, so I took them to events in Detroit with my own publicist so they could learn the business.

Against my better judgment, I also opened a second daycare in the same building. The kids were everywhere, and the church continued to receive funding—and I continued to receive nothing. As my business took off, I started getting a lot of negative attention. Due to external pressures and politics, people began to treat me poorly. My friends who worked at the daycare started to sabotage my business, not making corrections that inspectors required. They were purposely neglecting to document the corrective action plans. When I would ask if they had completed their tasks, they would lie and say yes.

I even tested them by giving each person different information to see who was talking behind my back. They also started doing a lot of strange things to keep tabs on me. Because they were hiding the corrective action mail, I wasn't getting the notices I needed, which ultimately led to me losing my daycare.

Due to the **negligence of my friends**—the people I trusted—I was losing my daycare. I felt like I was in the fight of my life. I had to quickly hire a lawyer to try and save the business while also fighting to stay in the building. I couldn't fight anymore.

The people who owned the building were pushing me out. To this day, I don't understand why they treated me so horribly. At the same time, they were investing in a home on the same property and asked me to turn it into a house for young girls. I agreed, but I needed guidance. I asked a woman who had successfully developed homes for men to help me. Unbeknownst to me, she was on the board for the very building my daycare was in. Soon after, they offered her the building and let her start her own group home for girls.

Looking back, I realize it was all politics, and I was being screwed over. My licenses weren't being renewed properly, and the licensing official was constantly citing my business for violations, even though I was doing everything right. They were all working together. To make matters worse, my staff started turning on me. These young women, in their early 20s, had never run a business but were telling me I didn't know what I was doing and actively sabotaging my work. It just shows how fast people will turn on you.

The girl who lived with me—the one I fed, clothed, and kept safe—had a mother whom I hired as my administrative assistant. She started feeding her daughter lies about my business, and her daughter then repeated them to my other employees, creating a huge mess. Hiring friends and people I knew destroyed my peace and my business. Everyone started looking at me like a failure, like I didn't know how to run my own company.

I was the one taking classes to improve, but they made it seem like I was doing everything wrong. All the while, my so-called friends were intentionally messing things up. They ignored my instructions, failed to interact with the children, and ruined my paperwork. I let too much slide when I shouldn't have. By the time I finally started being stern, it was too late. I lost my daycare for the second time.

When I lost my daycare the first time, I had to move fast. Within a week, I created a new LLC and EIN to keep my business running. But my new hires—more people I knew—also failed me. That's when I truly realized that the building owners and my employees didn't want me to succeed. My lawyer even said it didn't make sense and that it seemed like I was being attacked.

I think people might have seen me becoming too powerful in my work with the youth. I was earning so much respect and creating real change by teaching the youth financial literacy, preparing them for college, and giving them job readiness skills. I even took them on college tours without any funding or help from their parents.

Not only was I short on funding, but I also lacked a team that could help me reach the next level. I didn't have anyone with connections or who sat on a board who could help elevate my business and youth programs. It was sad how jealousy and envy led people to push my business out, simply because they thought I was getting grants and state money, not realizing the reality of what I was going through. With God's help, I funded everything myself.

Then, the pastor—the woman of God, supposedly—started doing and saying things to push me out, including telling me they were going to sell the building. They even used my mother's death against me, saying they didn't think I could handle it and needed time to grieve.

While I was at the building, I met a woman who ran a program to feed the homeless, and I often took my girls to volunteer. She told me she was about to move her program into the same building (the building that was supposedly up for sale) and that they were giving her funding and upgrading the kitchen for her. They were doing everything for her that they should have done for me.

After she heard my story, she felt so bad that she offered to buy my daycare equipment. The pastor had to give her the money to pay me. She told them she needed my supplies, and they agreed to pay. The funny part is, she didn't need any of it. She received $5,000 from them to pay me, not realizing that I had lost everything. I was so depressed that I made a social media post telling people that if they needed daycare equipment, they could buy it from me. I made another $6,000 from those sales.

In the end, she didn't take the building. She told me, "They did you so wrong that I couldn't take the building!" They had collected over a million dollars in PPP loans and other funding because my daycare was there. Her decision not to take the building felt like karma finally bite them in the butt.

When I look back at my finances, I can't believe that one year I made at least **$700,000** with both daycares and didn't see a dime of it. I had no financial structure, so I was giving money to everyone, funding my programs, and just spending. These people didn't care if I lived or died, and I was bending over backward for them.

I suffered in the long run, and I'll be damned if I make those mistakes again. When my mom passed away, half the community didn't even show up. I have a new circle of friends now and I am keeping my circle close. God revealed the intentions of a lot of people to me. He showed me who wasn't ready or able to continue this journey with me, because eventually, things were going to get better, and everyone isn't meant to be on this ride with me.

NOTES

Chapter 4

Resilience

Life started getting incredibly hard for me, especially during the pandemic in 2019 - 2021. I lost my mother-in-law, my mom, and then my husband 12 months later. It felt like life was taking its toll on me. To make things worse, the people I valued and trusted most stabbed me in the back, which led to my daycare being shut down. I felt so alone and depressed because of the betrayal and the recent losses. I was trying to maintain and run several businesses, all while watching them crumble. I just couldn't see a way to get past it.

What people fail to realize is that resilience is a superpower. Resilient can be defined as a person who is able to withstand or recover quickly from difficult situations, and I was that person. I used to cry myself to sleep and felt like I had made the biggest mistake of my life by chasing a dream. After the betrayal by my friends, I questioned if I could ever trust again. Most people in a similar situation might choose violence, but I didn't let it get that far.

I learned that **resilience isn't something you're born with; it's something you build over time.** I had to train my mind to see failures as "feedback from God" so he could help me get through and strengthen me in certain areas of my life. When my daycare shut down, I thought about crawling into a corner. But then I also thought about getting up to keep moving and show everyone that they weren't going to stop me. I will always find a way to keep pushing. I'll cry it out, but then I'll get up and keep moving.

I realized I had to shift my mindset and start growing both in my business and as a person. I began reading different books to change my mindset and learn about money, how to deal with people, and other things that helped me feel stronger. I'm thankful for books like *Rich Dad Poor Dad*, *The Psychology of Money*, and *The 50th Laws of Power*.

Reading and studying taught me not to trust everyone, not to hire friends and family, and to keep my personal life to a minimum. I've stopped sharing so much of my personal life, even on social media, because the evilness of people is transferable. Even if you aren't physically around people, when your life is spiritually connected and you have a strong relationship with God, you gain many gifts.

I had to completely reset my life because I felt like I was dying on the inside, falling apart.

Depression was winning; I started gaining weight and crying all the time. I was in a dark place where I dimmed my own light. I truly thought it was me against the world, which is not a healthy place to be.

That's when I realized I needed to be more spiritual and read more spiritual books. Once I was in a more spiritual place, it gave me clarity, and I was able to analyze things from a new perspective. Here is an exercise that I did, and I also did it with my youth group:

1. I wrote down all the people in my family (grandparents, parents, aunts, uncles, siblings, and cousins).

2. Next to each name, I wrote down their accomplishments.

When I did this, I realized that a lot of my family members did not have a college degree; some had a degree, and some worked a 9-to-5 job. I sat back and analyzed what everyone had and had not accomplished. This gave me a reality check and created a new desire in me to want more. It fueled me to add my own goals to the list, knowing that my accomplishments might one day inspire my kids, grandkids, and cousins.

Right now, my cousins (my mother's sisters' children) and I all have successful businesses, and we help each other out. We are extremely close, and I am probably the only one who has friends because we keep our circle tight. The friends I have now are on my level; they have the same mindset as me, and we are all going in the same direction. This showed me that everyone isn't meant to go where you are going, and you can't bring everyone with you. We can't save everyone. Sometimes we ignore our intuition because we want to save people. If I had listened to my intuition a long time ago, none of this would have happened.

Looking back, I remember my mom used to warn me about my so-called friends. She was able to read every person in my life, and everything she said came true, including what would happen with my building. Of course, I didn't listen because I was young and naive, but the wisdom of our parents and grandparents is solid because they have already lived that life. It might not have been the exact same way you are living, but they know. They would never steer you wrong, especially if their advice comes from a place of love.

With the wisdom I gained, I try to help those I am close to. In addition to all of that, I helped a girl who ended up stabbing me in the back. I kept questioning myself, asking, "What was her issue with me?" It was strange how everything in my life shut down at once. I had nothing at one point. I was living in my apartment and didn't know how I was going to pay the bills. I used my money to pay for my husband's funeral because no one would help me. I just shut down and didn't want to be here anymore. I felt as if everyone hated me, and all I was trying to do was live right and make a difference in my community.

Because I was so depressed and stayed in my room. I lost the daycare, but I technically didn't close it. Because I didn't do the corrective action plan, I lost my stars, and eventually, my kids fell off my roster, and I wasn't getting paid. The parents didn't realize that they were receiving free daycare services because the state hadn't paid me in a month. Again, I made a post on social media letting everyone know that I was selling my daycare supplies. I made $6,000 that day, which helped me pay my bills.

Things were happening to me left and right, and people had no idea what I was going through. I lost my car because it was in my husband's name. My basement was flooded for almost a year because two contractors I paid ran off with my money without doing the work. On top of all that, I was dead broke for a long time.

Meanwhile, I was still doing my podcast and conducting interviews while depressed. No one knew what I was going through because I held it all together, even though I was dying on the inside. I was uplifting others while knowing I didn't want to be here anymore. I still had people around me who were being nasty and rude for no reason, but no matter how I felt, I never retaliated. I just continued to be myself.

After the losses I experienced, I noticed people would say they will be there for me. But after two weeks, people went back to their normal lives, while I was left to grieve and pick up all the pieces. That's when reality started to kick in. Still, I was getting up at 5 a.m. for my first kid to come at 6 a.m., closing at midnight, and doing my podcast in between, all with no support. Publicists wouldn't let their clients post that they were on my show and were demanding and nasty. People had no idea what I was really going through.

NOTES

Chapter 5

Authenticity

I'm a firm believer in watching what I say and how I treat people, because you never know who you're talking to or how they might be able to help you in the future. I've seen people mistreat others so badly, not knowing that person could be a blessing to them. After being mistreated myself, I promised that I would never treat others that way.

People can get sidetracked by social media, where they make their lives look far more glamorous than they are. People fall for it and will mistreat you because you don't have a designer bag or live a certain lifestyle, unaware that these things can be fake, borrowed, or rented just for show. Because of this, I started to see many people differently. I decided to stay in my own lane and treat everyone right, always aligning myself with what is right.

Everything I do, from my podcast to my daily life, is built on authenticity. I don't sugarcoat anything; I'm just myself. It can be challenging, as some people expect me to live a glamorous lifestyle. I have a home, a car, and financial security, but I don't feel the need to flaunt it on social media or in real life. I'm blessed to have these things, and they represent a journey I began in my darkest moments.

I started by getting my finances in order, rebuilding my credit, and educating myself. I also had to regain my stars for my daycare, so I entered a childcare program that changed my life, thanks to Brittney. Now, I'm also in a program with the Akron Urban League, where I'm earning certifications, creating a financial plan, and securing loans. I was even recently awarded $2,000 by the mayor. "The shift is shifting!" This shows how things can change when you remain obedient to God. Even when people treat you poorly or things don't go your way, you can't give up on your faith. You have to pray it out.

I bought a Bible that helps me understand my feelings and what I'm going through, because I'm not good at reciting quotes—and that's okay. You have to be more spiritual. People don't realize how spiritual it is to run a business. You can either dance with the devil and be rewarded by him, or you can dance with God and be patient for blessings on His timing. When you do things His way, you will be blessed. I've had to do things His way, and now I want to educate people and change their mindset. Let people watch you be blessed in their faces. At one point, I felt cursed and unworthy, telling myself, "I'm never getting approved, and I'm never going to have good friends!" Doubt can creep up on you fast.

Learning to trust people again is scary. I used to think, "I don't want a business partner, they could turn on me!" But I had to shift my mindset and realize that sometimes it's good to have a partner. The key is to be aligned with the right people, and to do that, I had to heal myself first. I had to separate from the world and get into my own.

I began praying and doing my own Bible studies, talking with God. I started journaling a lot to understand my feelings, weighing the pros and cons of my life, and identifying what I needed to improve and what I needed to strengthen. I worked on myself so much that now, "I'm addicted to me!" I'm addicted to becoming the person I want to be–to a point where nobody can tell me shit about myself. I dug so deep within my soul and made sure to heal every part of me to become a better version of myself.

Now that I am truly healed and in the space where I need to be, God is sending genuine people to help me in so many ways. In the 17 years I've been a business owner, I've never heard people tell me that I'm powerful, dope, or amazing. It feels good to finally get compliments.

I've reached a point where I can feel when someone is trying to dim my light or is praying against me. This is a superpower you develop when you start working on yourself. I often hear women say they want the right man or that they're afraid of being lonely, but sis, you have to work on yourself first for God to send you the right person. The same principle applies to business. If you want a better business, you have to become a better person first, because your business represents you.

Lessons Learned for Business and Life

1. **Prioritize your time and your business.** Instead of putting so much trust in others, focus your energy on what truly matters: your business.

2. **Document everything.** Writing things down and recording meetings ensures you have a clear record of every decision and conversation.

3. **Protect your space.** Keep your personal life and accomplishments private and be selective about who you allow into your inner circle.

4. **Remove negativity immediately.** If someone is bringing drama or a bad attitude into your life or business, cut ties with them right away.

I had no business running my business the way I did. I let people play in my face, and it ultimately left me suffering. I got to a point where I couldn't even save myself. "I couldn't do CPR on my damn self!" It's truly a terrible feeling when two friends who hate each other are willing to come together just to plot against you. But if someone needs an entire army to take you down, that should be a sign of just how powerful you are. I learned that the hard way when people were coming for me from every direction.

NOTES

Chapter 6

Values

After everything I've been through—loss, grief, depression, and betrayal—I've learned to value myself and my life more than ever. I now focus on my present and my future, making sure every moment is spent with the people I love and doing things that bring me peace and happiness. I've worked too hard to let anyone interrupt my peace for two minutes, so I've learned to protect it fiercely.

I've also prioritized my health, which at one point I was neglecting. I was dealing with high blood pressure, pre-diabetes, and constant headaches. All I heard from people was, "She gained weight!" They had no idea what I was going through at the time, but I knew it was time to get my health in order.

When it comes to social media and my podcast, it seems women are often looking for a certain image: a fat ass, small waist, full makeup, and weave. If you aren't "glamorous," they aren't interested. People forget what you have been through and fail to give you grace. You're expected to look perfect every day, but that's not real life. Often, people who make you feel bad are only projecting how they feel about themselves.

I had to learn not to take everything personally. People will try to dump their problems on you and then blame you for being a mess, when in reality, you just absorbed their issues. I used to take on everyone else's problems without solving my own. I had to learn to separate the two. When someone felt a certain way about me, I realized it was their personal battle, not mine, because I know I am a good person.

I've learned that how a person feels about me is none of my business. Training myself not to take things personally was a huge weight lifted off my shoulders. My second language is now "no," and being able to say it has helped me immensely. In the last two years, I've saved more money than ever before. I used to give to everyone around me, but once I started saying no, I watched my income increase. Now that I see that increase, I want more for myself and to do more to help others.

People often don't understand that I'm trying to help them and put them in a better position. Instead, they want to play the victim and point the finger at everyone else. I've learned it's time to start pointing the finger at yourself. When 18-year-olds who have been adults for only a year started telling me I wasn't running my business correctly, I knew it was time for a change. It baffled me that they felt so entitled, and I had to cut them off.

I used to be angry at myself for becoming successful, but once I healed, I started getting excited about it because it helped people leave my life. Success helps you see people for who they are, and it's always the right people who end up disliking you. Once they remove themselves from your life, you no longer have to worry about them. For that, I thank success. It exposes people all the time because they are unable to keep their inner demons hidden.

I also feel that as a people, we should work on our emotional intelligence. It's needed because we often get too deep into our emotions and react impulsively. There's a difference between being emotionally intelligent and still being passionate about what you do. People can be disrespectful, and without emotional intelligence, you might react in a way that could hurt you in the long run. Because of your position in life, you can't just respond any way you want, as you may have a lot to lose.

I also had to learn to **shut the hell up**. People don't realize that silence is much louder than talking. You can learn so much more by listening. When people over-talk others and act like they know everything, they forget that there is always room to learn new things. Your silence and willingness to just listen can open so many doors for you. My silence has connected me with many amazing people. I've also noticed that it's been more white people assisting me than Black people.

I know not everyone wants to hear this, but it needs to be said: Why does our community feel like we have to be in competition with one another? I just don't understand it. For example, if I am the CEO of a company, and I have a vice president, the vice president wants to be the CEO. They may not be good at the CEO position, but because you have it, they just want it. Most people don't know how to stay in the lane where their gifts are. They always want to expand into another position that has nothing to do with their gifts. This mindset makes them not want anyone else to have that position. It shows how messed up the Black community's mindset is. We are programmed to be that way toward one another.

I felt this way when I was running my programs and daycares, and I feel it today when running my podcast. It feels like if you aren't in a certain social circle, selling your soul, kissing ass, or scamming, you can't get ahead. They make you feel as if you are not in the right groups when the only person you need on your team is **God**! When you have God, every door will open for you; there is no cheat code to this. A few people who treated me poorly are still in the same position in life they were in when they treated me poorly. People would rather tear you down than learn from you or other people. You can get further in life if you mind your business, stay in your own lane, work out, and eat clean.

NOTES

Chapter 7

Life Style Change

I've completely changed my life, and it feels great. Once you figure out the main tools or direction you want to go, you can become a millionaire. Think about many millionaires you see; they aren't wearing flashy chains or brand-name clothes. They might have a nice watch, but they often drive practical cars like a Subaru, Honda, or Toyota.

I've set financial goals to become a millionaire by a certain age. I continue to put myself in a better financial position by educating myself on crypto and stocks and ensuring I have an IRA. I'm also preparing for retirement and have the right whole-life insurance policy. I've even set up a trust.

Instead of endlessly scrolling through social media or apps that don't educate me, I make sure to read and learn. Our priorities are out of order, and we have to get our lives straight. There are so many unhealed people out there whose priorities are focused on other people's problems instead of seeking God and a therapist to start healing.

I feel like God is separating people, good versus evil, as people are being exposed left and right. We are starting to see influencers and celebrities for who they really are. They don't have it all together like they post. I feel like many of them are praying and seeking God, but I also feel like some are using God for a platform.

It's time to get your life in order and position yourself both financially and mentally. I cannot stress that enough. You can't think like a millionaire once a week and expect millionaire results; you have to **live like it daily**. Make it a routine.

When I played basketball, we had a routine before every practice and on game days. That experience helped me create a daily routine for my life. In the morning, before I even touch my phone, I do my morning affirmations. I speak life into myself before anyone has the chance to speak over me. I read a Bible verse as I write down different affirmations. I drink juice, coffee, or tea, then I work out for 30 minutes. I take time out for myself, and then I spend five minutes visualizing how I want my day and life to look. I visualize what I want; for example, I once dreamt about going to Africa, and I made it happen.

Journaling has become a big part of my life. Every day, I write down and thank God for three wins from the previous day, no matter how small they were. I also use strategic planning, choosing three priority tasks for the day. I only do three because I don't want to overwhelm myself. For instance, my goal was to fix my credit, and it took me a year, but I did something toward that goal every day. You have to commit for 21 days to change your mindset and create a routine that will help you achieve your goals.

I read for 10 minutes a day to expand my mindset and listen to different podcasts, including my own, to gain knowledge. When you write something down, it makes more sense. "Write the vision and make it plain." I want people to shift their mindset to one of abundance, believing that there is enough business for everyone.

My business is in childcare, so I had to shift my mindset on different ways to advertise and get new clients. Instead of just posting on social media, I made flyers (the old-school way), used Google ads, and went through the Better Business Bureau. I focused on my own business because once you start looking at what others are doing, you cloud your own vision. I am not in competition with anyone because I mind the business that pays me, so I share my resources with other business owners. I love blessing others because when you bless others, you will be blessed tenfold.

I've also learned to invest in myself without feeling guilty. I used to go to the store, fill up a cart, and then leave it all behind because I felt guilty. But if I shopped for others, I was happy and would buy up the whole store. I had to stop feeling guilty about investing in myself. Our minds are very busy every day, and we have to find time to relax them. You have to find a routine that works for you to calm the noise and focus on bettering yourself. When you get into a healthy routine, you move differently. You find yourself happier; you can feel the happiness. You will think to yourself, "I should have been doing this a long time ago!" It will motivate you to keep pushing and continue to upgrade your life.

$$2+2=4$$

$$x = \frac{-b \pm \sqrt{b^2 - 4ac}}{2a}$$

The Millionaire Mindset Playbook

$$\$$$

$$y = mx + b$$

People often fixate on the financial success they see, but this focus is precisely why I prioritize sharing my personal journey. What they don't see is the immense amount of unseen work, struggle, and sacrifice involved. The reality is that the financial rewards and perceived lifestyle often take **15, 20, or even 30 years to build.**

My goal is to show you the reality of building and maintaining a business. This is precisely why having a strategic playbook is non-negotiable. Like an underdog sports team, you will face losses and operate in obscurity for a while; you won't reach your full potential until the market truly recognizes you. Success, therefore, requires you to focus on what's going on within you—your strategy and growth—rather than simply worrying about the external competition.

The state of your physical environment is often a direct reflection of your internal mindset.

When your home is cluttered, it creates a corresponding **mental clutter** that inhibits clarity and focus. You cannot think properly or build a strategic business when your immediate environment is in disarray.

Consider this principle in other areas, such as vehicle maintenance: neglecting one small issue can trigger a **domino effect** that eventually leads to a catastrophic malfunction. It is the **act of neglect**, not the initial dirt or single small problem, that allows the crisis to build.

Too often, people allow small problems—in their business, finances, or personal life—to build up unaddressed. They look around and wonder why their life seems to be crumbling, but the reality is that the collapse is simply the result of long-term failure to **face the problem and take corrective action.**

Success is not solely measured by wealth. You can achieve massive financial success and still feel deeply unfulfilled or depressed if you have not **healed from past traumas**. This is fundamentally a psychological and spiritual matter. To navigate the complexities of life and sustain success, you must have a foundational **spiritual or personal belief system** in place. The lack of this inner peace is evident in the many people who achieve success yet remain unhappy. This realization is why I created my **10 Non-Negotiables for Entrepreneurial Success.** These are not mere suggestions; they are the pillars and governing laws I live by to remain steady, no matter how tough the business journey becomes.

THE MILLIONAIRE MINDSET PLAYBOOK

You've walked with me through a journey of breakthroughs and challenges. Now, it's time to take everything you've learned and put it into action.

The **Millionaire Mindset** isn't just about wealth in the bank. It's about building abundance in your faith, your peace, your time, and your relationships. When your peace, purpose, and profits work in harmony, you don't just have success—you find true freedom.

This playbook is the blueprint to get you there

The 10 Non-Negotiables for Entrepreneurial Success

These are not suggestions. These are the laws I live by now, the pillars that keep me steady no matter how tough business gets.

1. **PROTECT YOUR PEACE:** If it costs your mental health, it's too expensive. Learn to walk away from any deal, person, or opportunity that disturbs your spirit. **Peace is profit.** You must protect your internal power; if you cannot control your own well-being, you cannot fulfill your purpose. A lack of self-love and self-knowledge makes people vulnerable—and their energy available—to those with negative intentions. A person who doesn't love themselves cannot truly connect with or compare to someone who does. Remember this: if you leave your own broken pieces unfixed or expose them carelessly, others may see and use those vulnerabilities against you. **Always protect your peace.**

2. **NEVER STOP LEARNING:** The world changes fast, and what you knew last year may not be enough this year. **Books, podcasts, mentors, and courses are your essential armor.** Staying relevant demands that you remain **teachable**—you can never know everything. Seek out and connect with positive influencers who inspire you to grow and become the best version of yourself. True learning often happens when you are quiet and simply listen. Beyond words, you can learn a tremendous amount by observing people's **body language and communication styles**; these subtle cues offer deep insight.

3. **SEPARATE YOUR MONEY: Business and personal finances do not mix. Ever.** If you fail to respect your money, your money won't respect you. I learned this lesson firsthand with my non-profit organization: I was pouring capital into the venture, yet I lacked full control and awareness of my finances. I was spending money I didn't have and prioritizing others, which often left me vulnerable. Too many people depleted my resources and eventually left when I was no longer beneficial to them. Now, by **separating my personal and business accounts**, I have clear visibility into where every dollar goes. I recommend utilizing tools like QuickBooks, which uses AI-generated data to automatically categorize expenses and provide essential financial clarity.

4. **SAY "NO" WITHOUT QUILT: Your "yes" is valuable currency–protect it.** Every "yes" you give to something that doesn't align with your purpose takes you one step further from your own goals. The hard reality is that some people will use you until you have nothing left to offer. You must develop **discernment** to see people for who they truly are. Set firm **boundaries** on what you give to others, because entitlement is real. When you give too much, you devalue yourself. That individual will no longer see your efforts as hard work on your part, but as something you are *required* to do for them. Your efforts stop serving your destiny and start serving theirs.

5. **HIRE SLOW, FIRE FAST!** The wrong people can swiftly drain your energy, money, and reputation. **Do not hesitate to let them go.** One toxic employee or partnership can undo years of hard work. You have to actively protect your business–your "baby." I learned the hard way: I saw problems transpiring early on but waited too long to act. That delay cost me thousands in payroll taxes and caused significant damage. As soon as you feel that misalignment, **execute the necessary shift immediately.** Don't sit around waiting for everything to fall apart.

6. **DOCUMENT EVERYTHING: Document absolutely everything.** Every agreement, partnership, or payment should be in writing, not based on verbal trust. Verbal promises disappear, but **contracts protect you.** This rule applies to everyone, including friends, family, and new business partners. You'll thank yourself later for having clear contracts and legal counsel in place. Sadly, people can and will betray your trust. They may switch up or play dumb to avoid accountability. To protect yourself and your business–your hard work–from ruin, always keep a meticulous paper trail. If things feel off, ensure you have documented evidence, whether that's a contract, an email, or a dated note detailing the conversation.

7. **PAY YOURSELF FIRST:** You are not just a worker in your business; **you are the owner.** Owners don't starve while everyone else eats. Value yourself enough to take your deserved portion. Specifically, you must **add yourself to payroll**–this is a non-negotiable step that offers significant future financial benefits. To ensure compliance and proper structure, **hire an accountant** to manage your payroll and, most importantly, **pay your taxes** correctly and on time.

8. **BUILD RELATIONSHIPS, NOT JUST SALES:** While some people operate with a transactional, "salesy" approach, the truth is that **sales are transactional, but relationships are transformational.** The right connections can open doors that no amount of money can buy. This can be challenging for those who, like me, struggle with trust and require time to warm up. However, it is vital to be deliberate about who you allow into your circle. Don't just *know* people casually; take the time to know them **internally, mentally, and spiritually.** This deep knowledge will safeguard you from the heartache caused by their future actions. While some people can't change who they are, **you control where you place them.** Understand that every person in your life

deserves a different level of space and conversation based on their true character. Having celebrity friends means little; having a strong support system where you operate as a reciprocal team is what truly matters.

9. **RUN ON SYSTEMS, NOT CHAOS:** While **hustle builds a business, systems sustain it.** If everything falls apart the moment you step away, you don't own a business—you simply own a stressful job. Self-care is essential: neglect of your mental, physical, or emotional well-being will lead to burnout and failure. To maintain balance, you must create consistent operating systems. Furthermore, invest in your support network: secure a **spiritual advisor, a business mentor, and a close circle of like-minded friends.** As you level up and grow, you'll need to continually shift that circle, as not everyone can understand or support your evolving success.

10. **STAY ALIGNED WITH YOUR PURPOSE: No deal is worth selling your soul.** If an opportunity doesn't align with your core values, let it go. True wealth is built on something you can be proud of, and staying true to yourself will always be the ultimate win. Your unique identity is your power; no one else can be you. When you fully grasp that truth, prosperity naturally follows. It's crucial to understand that knowing your worth and the value of your hard work is more important than any contract or paycheck. Never become desperate for a deal simply because it presents an "opportunity." Working with a celebrity or a top company shouldn't matter; **your integrity and value** are your highest assets.

The Millionaire Mindset Affirmations

This declaration is your anchor—your steadfast defense against the inevitable days when **fear, scarcity, or betrayal** try to shake your foundation. Say it until you fully believe it.

- I am building a life, not just a business.

- I protect my peace as fiercely as my profits.

- I am disciplined with God, myself, money, time, and energy.

- I welcome opportunities that align with my mission and release those that don't.

- I am unstoppable in the face of challenges because I know they'll bless & shape me.

- I don't chase. I attract through excellence, integrity, and consistency.

- I am not afraid to say no, to walk away, or to start again.

- I am creating impact, leaving a legacy, and building wealth that outlives me.

- I move in faith. I work in excellence. My success is inevitable.

START, STOP & CONTINUE FRAMEWORK

The **"Start, Stop, Continue" framework** is a simple yet powerful system designed to help individuals and businesses clarify their path and refine their strategy.

1. **START** adding habits which will grow you:

    a. Weekly money reviews.

    b. Networking with intention.

    c. Journaling wins.

Too often, we overlook our victories because we are excessively hard on ourselves. We fail to pause and truly appreciate **how much we've been "poppin our shit" and how long we've been succeeding.** Take a moment to recognize your resilience and celebrate the wins you've already secured.

2. **STOP** activities and habits that drain you.

    a. Operating without contracts.

    b. Funding others while neglecting yourself.

    c. Chasing clout.

3. **CONTINUE** reinforcing what already works.

    a. Invest in personal growth.

    b. Staying consistent.

    c. Protecting your peace.

    d. Putting yourself first.

    e. Making your business better.

We must continually monitor current trends and market changes to understand how to effectively **pivot and adapt our business strategies.** These strategic adjustments are essential for reducing overwhelm and maintaining efficiency.

The 90-Day Millionaire Mindset Challenge

Change doesn't come from big leaps. It comes from small, daily steps that add up.

For the next 90 days:

1. Choose 3 financial habits - e.g., set aside tax money weekly, pay yourself first, or review all expenses every Sunday.

2. Choose 3 mindset habits - e.g., morning affirmations, journaling gratitude, or speaking one bold declaration over your life daily.

3. Choose 3 business habits - e.g., networking weekly, creating SOPs, or following up with every lead.

Do them daily for 90 days. By the end, your discipline will be stronger, your systems clearer, and your confidence is unshakable

The Big Reminder

The Millionaire Mindset is not perfection, it's consistency.

You will stumble. You will make mistakes. But you no longer start from zero. You start from experience.

Every time you come back to this playbook, you strengthen your resilience, your systems, and your belief that you are built for this.

MONTH 1: Faith & Foundation (Days 1–30)

1. Faith is the currency that opens doors money can't buy.

2. Your mind is the soil; plant words of abundance, not weeds of doubt.

3. God will never give you a vision without giving you provision.

4. A millionaire shift begins with a mustard seed of faith.

5. Don't chase success, chase alignment.

6. Prayer is strategy in motion.

7. Your words create wealth long before your hands touch it.

8. When God is your CEO, losses become lessons, not endings.

9. Legacy begins in your heart before it shows up in your bank account.

10. Build with God first; everything else will follow.

11. Fear is loud; faith is steady, listen to the steady.

12. What you believe about yourself sets your income ceiling.

13. Your circle is a soil plant yourself where you can grow.

14. Wealth without wisdom becomes waste.

15. Gratitude multiplies what's already in your hands.

16. Let go of people who limit your vision; they can't afford your future.

17. Prayer opens doors hustle could never unlock.

18. Abundance is a mindset, not a dollar amount.

19. Don't pray for tables, pray for wisdom to build them.

20. If you want God-sized results, you need God-sized faith.

21. Your mindset is the engine; your habits are the fuel.

22. You can't heal in the same environment that broke you.

23. Silence the noise so you can hear the assignment.

24. You can't walk into a millionaire mindset with a victim spirit.

25. God doesn't call the qualified He qualifies the called.

26. Wealth follows obedience, not shortcuts.

27. You're not broke, you're just in seed time.

28. A renewed mind attracts renewed opportunities.

29. Prosperity is peace, purpose, and provision working together.

30. Every test is a setup for your testimony.

MONTH 2: Money & Abundance (Days 31–60)

31. You don't need more money; you need more discipline.

32. Stop praying for wealth while mismanaging what's already in your hands.

33. Rich is a moment; wealth is a mindset.

34. Every dollar is a soldier; send it to fight for your freedom.

35. Abundance comes to those who honor their assignments.

36. Stewardship today secures legacy tomorrow.

37. Millionaires don't avoid risk, they manage it wisely.

38. Saving is protection; investing is multiplication.

39. Wealthy people think in decades, not days.

40. Money is a magnifier that reveals who you already are.

41. A poor mindset wastes, a rich mindset spends, a wealthy mindset multiplies.

42. Wealth starts with what you believe you deserve.

43. Budgeting is telling your money where to go instead of wondering where it went.

44. Financial freedom is the fruit of daily choices, not lottery tickets.

45. Every unnecessary expense steals from your legacy.

46. Money flows where clarity grows.

47. Don't just earn income, build impact.

48. Luxury without legacy is emptiness.

49. Invest in assets, not appearances.

50. Wealth whispers; poverty screams.

51. Don't let instant gratification rob you of long-term elevation.

52. Millionaires create money systems; broke people chase money.

53. The goal isn't to look rich, it's to stay wealthy.

54. Money is not evil, it's a tool in the hands of purpose.

55. Financial peace is louder than material things.

56. Pay yourself first, or you'll always be last.

57. Build wealth quietly, live abundantly loudly.

58. Every dollar saved is a brick in your freedom.

59. Stop chasing likes and start chasing legacy.

60. Real abundance is being debt-free, stress-free, and purpose-filled.

MONTH 3: Resilience & Growth (Days 61–90)

61. Diamonds form under pressure so do legacies.

62. Every "no" you hear is God's protection, not rejection.

63. Don't fear failure, fear staying the same.

64. Comfort zones are where dreams go to die.

65. Millionaires master patience before profits.

66. Endurance is a millionaire's secret weapon.

67. Pain produces power if you don't quit.

68. Setbacks are setups for elevation.

69. Don't bury your gifts in excuses.

70. Growth costs comfort but pays freedom.

71. What broke you yesterday is building you today.

72. Millionaire habits look boring to average minds.

73. Keep planting seeds even when the soil looks dry.

74. If you don't quit, you can't lose.

75. Every loss is tuition for wisdom.

76. The climb is lonely, but the view is legacy.

77. Don't rush the process God is still writing your story.

78. Rejection redirects you to where you belong.

79. Don't compare your chapter 3 to someone's chapter 30.

80. Discipline is the bridge between dreams and destiny.

81. Millionaires wake up with purpose, not problems.

82. Don't shrink to fit, expand to lead.

83. The hardest battles produce the strongest leaders.

84. Winners see obstacles as opportunities.

85. Your consistency will outperform their talent.

86. Millionaires don't wait for motivation, they build discipline.

87. Resilience is wealth you can't lose.

88. Don't pray for an easier life, pray for stronger shoulders.

89. The storm is temporary, but your growth is permanent.

90. You are not your past, you are your progress.

Building Financial Armor

One of the **hardest truths I faced as an entrepreneur** wasn't making money—it was realizing that making it isn't enough. You have to know how to **keep it, grow it, and protect it.**

Early on, I was addicted to the chase—believing that more clients and more cash was the ultimate flex. I didn't realize that a brand can look like a million bucks on Instagram while crumbling internally. I learned that lesson the expensive way, costing me $60,000 to realize that without structure, your 'success' is just a high-priced illusion.

This isn't about shame; it's about building the **financial armor** you need so your business can survive storms, betrayal, bad deals, and even your own generosity.

WHY FINANCIAL STRUCTURE MATTERS

I'll be honest: I truly believed establishing an LLC and getting an EIN meant I had "arrived" as a serious business owner. What I didn't realize was the complexity of the ongoing compliance—quarterly taxes, license renewals, payroll reports, and how fast missed deadlines could financially cripple a new venture.

When you're focused on the hustle, paperwork feels like the ultimate distraction. But neglecting it means you're building your business on sand. When the storm comes, those simple oversights will wash away everything you worked for.

Truth: **Structure isn't boring; it's your essential safety net.**

When I first launched my childcare business, I was highly successful at generating revenue, but I lacked the crucial skills to **strategize, grow, and organize** that money. I naively assumed that establishing an LLC and securing an EIN was the extent of my financial obligations. Nobody educated me on the essential knowledge required to scale the business and, most importantly, **stop spending personal money on business expenses.** I later learned the true power of maintaining excellent personal credit (like a 700+ score) as a foundation for securing crucial business credit. Understanding how to leverage both **personal capital** (funds generated from high revenue) and **external capital** (such as business credit cards or lines of credit) is the key to sustainable financial growth.

I lacked this financial knowledge because I simply wasn't educated on business fundamentals. If I had known then what I know now, I could have progressed much further, securing high-limit credit balances, perhaps even in the **$25,000 to $100,000 range**.

This lack of knowledge cost me dearly, particularly when I lost my second daycare center. At that time, I accumulated **$225,000 in tax liens**—a debt I didn't even know existed until I attempted to secure a later loan.

I discovered that mistakes had been made on my Schedule C tax filings. My records indicated I hadn't filed taxes in five years. Because I wrongly assumed everything was being submitted correctly, I wasn't double-checking my accountant's work. I ultimately had to go back and file the correct paperwork, which successfully reduced my debt liability from $225,000 to only **$50,000.**

When starting a business, it's vital to know it's not enough to simply have an LLC or incorporation. You must immediately establish a solid business foundation built on structure, discipline, and education. To protect yourself and your assets, you must seek proper, credible education and guard against scams. Avoid running with every tip you read online or hear on a podcast. Instead, always check the credentials of your source and verify their legitimacy. Go to local professionals, ask specific questions, and commit to the research necessary to become a genuine business owner. Through my own research, I discovered crucial steps like obtaining a DUNS number to build a business credit profile and navigating specific local certifications (like Ohio's MBE, WBE, DBE, and EDGE programs).

A **DUNS Number** (which stands for **Data Universal Numbering System**) is a unique nine-digit identifier for businesses, created and maintained by the credit reporting agency **Dun & Bradstreet (D&B)**.

MBE is a widely used business certification acronym that stands for **Minority Business Enterprise**. It is a certification granted to businesses that are majority-owned, operated, and controlled by members of specific minority groups.

The acronym **WBE** stands for **Women's Business Enterprise**, the WBE certification is designed to promote and provide opportunities for businesses majority-owned and controlled by women.

The acronym **DBE** stands for **Disadvantaged Business Enterprise**. This is a specific certification program established and regulated by the U.S. Department of

Transportation (DOT). It is primarily focused on promoting opportunities in federally funded transportation infrastructure projects.

The acronym **EDGE** typically refers to a specific state-level certification program in the United States, most notably the **Encouraging Diversity, Growth, and Equity (EDGE)** program in **Ohio**.

I want to emphasize that these essential details—like state programs and certifications—were things I had to learn through self-education. My research revealed the many resources and programs available right here in my state, prompting me to immediately file the necessary paperwork.

This is why I urge every entrepreneur to **prioritize setting up a strong business foundation** and, crucially, to **maintain a comprehensive paper trail** for everything. Too many business owners mix personal and business funds due to a lack of structure, leading to financial chaos and missed opportunities.

Separate Your Money or Lose It All

One of the biggest mistakes I made early on was treating my business bank account like a personal piggy bank, rationalizing it by thinking, "It's all my money anyway."

I was completely wrong.

When you commingle personal and business funds, you invite severe consequences:

- **You lose clarity:** It becomes impossible to accurately track profitability.

- **Taxes become a nightmare:** Tax season turns into a messy, complicated process.

- **You risk everything:** You expose yourself to legal and liability risks (piercing the corporate veil)

When managing your business finances, **structure is non-negotiable.** You must maintain complete separation between your personal and business funds, which requires dedicated personal and business checking and savings accounts. In fact, you may even need multiple business accounts—I personally use two: one exclusively for payroll and a second for handling deposits and managing all operational bills.

To maintain clarity and compliance, connect accounting software like **QuickBooks** to your business checking account. This allows you to effortlessly categorize transactions, track profits and losses, and maintain a clear ledger of all income and expenses. This meticulous record-keeping is not optional; it is the **precise documentation (profit, loss, and gains)** you must provide when applying for certifications.

Business savings accounts are important, I can't count the number of times a business crisis hit, leaving me scrambling for money I didn't have. That kind of financial stress will truly age you before your time.

Today, I operate with peace of mind by maintaining a business emergency fund equal to **three to six months of operating expenses.** This strategic reserve means that if clients pay late, a major piece of equipment breaks, or the economy unexpectedly slows down, I am insulated from panic mode.

Action Tip: Start small. Even setting aside $50 a week into a separate savings account will build a powerful safety net over time.

Action Steps for Financial Structure

To implement immediate financial separation and clarity:

- **Open separate accounts:** Establish a dedicated business checking account and a business savings account.

- **Implement bookkeeping:** Start using a reliable bookkeeping tool such as **QuickBooks, Wave, or FreshBooks.**

- **Schedule a review:** Commit to a weekly "money date" to review all income and expenses and maintain up-to-date records.

THE PAY-YOURSELF RULE

For years, I made the costly mistake of pouring every dollar back into my business or dedicating it to helping others. While that generosity was well-intentioned, it ultimately left me broke.

The truth is: Paying yourself is not selfish—it is essential for long-term sustainability.

Here is my current compensation strategy:

- **20% of revenue goes directly to me as the owner.**

- **30% is immediately set aside for taxes.**

- The remaining percentage covers all operating expenses, payroll, and growth initiatives.

Even if you can only start with $50 a week, pay yourself something. This builds the critical habit and reinforces the mindset that you are not just an operator—you are the owner.

Every sustainable business needs a formal payroll system to properly compensate both **staff and the owner.** While many business owners resist payroll due to the immediate tax implications (which we will detail in the next section), paying yourself correctly is the single most critical step for your personal financial success and business growth.

It is essential to understand that paying yourself is not just an expense; it is a strategic step in **building your personal wealth and creditworthiness.**

When seeking major personal loans, such as for buying a home or expanding property, lenders primarily look at your verifiable **personal income**, not your business revenue. High business revenue without clear personal income will hinder your approval chances.

To ensure verifiable income and fuel expansion, paying yourself is extremely critical. A smart range for owner compensation is **30% to 50% of your net profit.**

Net Profit Example: $200,000/year	Annual Pay	Monthly Pay (Approx.)
30% Pay Rate	**$60,000/year**	**$5,000/month**
40% Pay Rate	**$80,000/year**	**$6,667/month**
50% Pay Rate	**$100,000/year**	**$8,333/month**

To expand your business and secure outside financing, you must establish verified income through formal methods like W-2s or clear Owner Distributions. Always aim for a low Debt-to-Income (DTI) ratio, ideally below 43%, as this is what lenders use to approve your personal financial applications.

Building your business and your wealth requires strong **business credit**. Start by securing your **DUNS Number**, and then use a platform like **Nav.com** to effectively manage your credit profile. When offered the Nav credit card, ensure all your foundational documents are in place. They may provide an initial spending limit (e.g., $95) to encourage immediate use and repayment, which immediately helps build your history. For specific industries, like contracting, utilizing vendors such as **Quill** and ensuring they report to the credit bureaus is another excellent way to boost business credit.

Stop focusing on your personal lifestyle and impressing others; dedicate that energy to building your business credit instead. Real success takes time: it typically requires **5 to 10 years** to fully establish your structure exactly as you want it, with the tenth year often marking a significant flourishing period. Finally, learn to identify your slow and peak seasons. During your busy season, save aggressively to carry you through the slow periods. I've personally strategized to the point where I no longer experience a true "down season."

Achieving financial freedom requires discipline across several key areas:

1. Debt and Credit Discipline

- Always pay your bills on time.

- Maintain personal credit card usage below **30% of your available limit** (never max out your cards).

2. Savings and Liquidity

- Utilize a **High-Yield Savings Account (HYSA)** to earn monthly interest on your reserves.

- Build an emergency fund covering **3 to 6 months of both business and personal income.**

3. Investment and Growth

- Learn to put your money to work. Educate yourself on core investments like **Stocks, Bonds, and ETFs**. You can also explore digital assets like cryptocurrency.

- **Resource Tip:** YouTube channels featuring experts like Chris Sain and Sierra Aaliyah are great resources for foundational stock market education.

- **Real Estate:** This is another powerful source of income. Consider owning land, acquiring rental properties, or investing in different property types. (I personally love the security of owning my home outright, ensuring I have equity for emergencies.)

4. Retirement and Legacy

- **Entrepreneurs must plan their own retirement** since they don't have traditional employer-matched accounts.

- Open a **ROTH IRA** immediately. You can invest in stocks and crypto within this account. If you have an old 401k from a previous job, consider rolling it over into your ROTH IRA.

These strategic steps ensure your money is channeled into the correct places, allowing you to build sustainable wealth and secure your future.

TAXES WILL CATCH UP TO YOU

I learned this essential lesson the hard way: **Ignoring or postponing taxes is like trying to hide from the sun—it will catch you eventually.**

To secure your financial future, follow these essential **Key Steps:**

1. **Fund a Reserve:** Set aside a percentage of every dollar earned immediately into a dedicated tax savings account.

2. **Hire an Expert:** Find a tax professional who specializes in small business finances, not just standard personal returns.

3. **Prioritize Deadlines:** Mark quarterly tax deadlines on your calendar and treat them as non-negotiable, VIP business appointments.

This is your financial armor: paying taxes on time is the single greatest way to ensure you stay in business and out of compliance trouble.

As previously emphasized, dedicating a separate account for taxes is mandatory. As a business owner, you are responsible for several layers of tax payments:

1. **Federal Payroll Taxes:** This includes Forms **941 and 940** for Social Security, Medicare, and Federal Unemployment Tax (FUTA).

2. **State Taxes:** These payments are often due monthly or quarterly, depending on your state's requirements.

3. **Local City Taxes:** This includes local business income tax and local unemployment taxes.

These tax obligations accrue quickly, and you must treat the money reserved for them as **untouchable.** To avoid a large, overwhelming bill, I recommend paying taxes **weekly or monthly.** Failure to keep up with payroll taxes can lead to serious consequences, including large debts owed to the IRS and debilitating tax liens. I personally pay my taxes monthly to keep the payments manageable.

Remember, business success requires patience—you must crawl before you walk. Don't rush to look successful; instead, invest in the correct structure. Without this financial foundation, your business will eventually crumble. Entrepreneurs who are self-employed must ensure their records and numbers meticulously match their tax filings. Find the compliance system that works best for your business.

CONTRACTS ARE NON-NEGOATIABLE

When starting out, it's tempting to rely on handshake deals with friends or people you "trust." But **trust, unfortunately, doesn't protect you in court.**

Now, I do not engage in any professional action without a comprehensive written agreement—and neither should you. This includes:

- Vendor contracts

- Employee/independent contractor agreements

- Partnership MOUs (Memorandums of Understanding)

- Client service agreements

A contract doesn't signal distrust; it is the essential framework that **protects the relationship** by establishing clear, documented expectations for all parties involved.

When lending money—or doing business, period—I don't care if it's your mother, cousin, or best friend: **make them sign on the dotted line.**

Some people take offense to being asked to sign a contract, but that offense often tells you everything you need to know about their intent. When someone resists a formal agreement, it suggests they either lack the intention to pay you back or disrespect the professional nature of the transaction.

Why Contracts are Non-Negotiable

Regardless of whether you are self-employed or work a 9-to-5, get that signature. People should respect this practice because it protects both parties. A contract is vital for:

- **Legal Protection:** It serves as a necessary legal tool.
- **Business Structure:** It enforces professional discipline.
- **Clear Expectations:** It defines exactly what is expected from the person signing the agreement.

Many feel they don't need to pay you back because they perceive you are "well off," or they feel justified in missing payments because they think you won't miss the money. But that is not how business works. **I need all my coins!**

The Importance of Thick Skin and Privacy

You must develop thick skin and realize that not everyone belongs in your business sphere. The people closest to you are often the first ones to take advantage. Protecting your money, maintaining your private space, and focusing on your own well-being are essential for success. **Your mental health and mindset must be right to lead your business, and that requires strong boundaries.**

STOP FUNDING YOUR OWN DOWNFALL

Here is the hardest pill I ever had to swallow: **Some of the deepest financial holes I fell into were dug by my own hands.**

I operated without boundaries. I gave out too many "favors" without protective contracts. I overpaid staff who demonstrated no respect for their roles. I funded the dreams of friends while my own business was actively sinking.

That wasn't generosity—it was **self-sabotage.** You must learn the crucial difference between helping others and hurting yourself. Your business cannot possibly serve others if it is drowning in the debt created by your own poor judgment.

Running a business is a **profound and transformative experience.** In the beginning, you are fueled by happiness and passion, eager to reach out for support and build a community. However, as time passes and you achieve progress, you will likely find yourself pulling away, preferring solitude and self-reliance.

This withdrawal is often the result of experiencing **pain and betrayal** in both your personal and business life. Yet, these experiences grant you a kind of superpower: sharpened **discernment.** You quickly learn to sense when someone is not genuine, distinguishing between authentic and harmful relationships.

Your failures and blessings are the lessons that will save you in the future. Though your path may feel lonely or painful now, in the end, it will all make sense. These hard-won lessons are necessary, ensuring you are better prepared to handle any challenges that try to resurface.

In closing: **Money without management is a trap.** You can spend years building a beautiful brand, only to end up with nothing to show for it if you fail to protect your finances. Financial armor doesn't just keep your business alive—it keeps **you in control.** And control, my friend, is the real power behind the millionaire mindset.

NOTES

My Why – The Woman Who Built My Millionaire Mindset"

Before you close this book, I want you to understand the heartbeat behind every word I've written and every lesson I've shared. The Millionaire Mindset Shift did not begin with me. It began with a woman whose strength could not be measured by titles or money my mother, **Sherice Thompson**.

My mother worked for the City of Akron for decades, doing some of the hardest labor you can imagine. She laid asphalt in the summer heat. She drove salt trucks through brutal snowstorms. She worked with her hands, her body, and her faith. And for years, she wasn't even a permanent employee.

In **1979**, her hourly wage was **$4.43**.

Year after year, she returned to the same job as a **seasonal worker**, laid off over and over again, never guaranteed stability, benefits, or security. Yet she showed up. She kept going. She refused to quit.

From 1979 through 1990, her raises came in **pennies**, not dollars.

$4.43 → $5.75 → $5.95 → $6.16.

She didn't become permanent until she was earning around **$8.50**.

In **1994**, she finally made **$11.28**.
In **1995**, she earned **$12.47**.
In **1998**, she reached **$12.84**.
By **1999**, she was making **$13.28 per hour**.

And yet, despite those wages, despite the layoffs, despite the instability and the physical toll of her work, my mother built wealth the best way she could. She purchased **two homes** one for me and one for my brother ensuring that her children would have something solid beneath their feet long after she was gone.

She didn't have a financial advisor.
She didn't have social media gurus.

She didn't have online courses.
She didn't have investment groups.

But she had discipline.
She had strategy.
She had wisdom.
She had credit she knew how to leverage.
And she had a vision for her children.

My brother and I never went without anything. My mother made sure of that. Even while she struggled with reading and literacy, she never struggled with understanding how to survive and build. She made sacrifices silently. She never complained. She simply worked, prayed, and provided. Single mother raising her two children. She let us be kids and never put us in "grown folk" business to where we felt the need to help her financially and more throughout the house. Which was a blessing.

My mother retired on **April 30, 2018** after dedicating her life to her job. But she never got the chance to enjoy the retirement she earned. She passed away on **October 25, 2019**, only one year later, from congestive heart failure.

Forty years of labor.
Eighteen months to rest.

That reality changed me forever.
It became the foundation of why I fight so hard today.
Why I refuse to settle.
Why I build wealth intentionally.
Why I teach others how to shift their mindset.

Because I watched my mother give everything to a job that could never repay her for the life she poured into it.

Even her life insurance – which was **$50,000** during her working years – was cut down to **$25,000** at retirement. Just like that. And if she didn't have a separate policy, we would have been left with nothing.

Her story is a reminder that one income stream is not security.

A job is not security.

Even retirement is not guaranteed.

This is why I teach that wealth is not just money.

Wealth is time.

Wealth is freedom.

Wealth is health.

Wealth is choice.

Wealth is preparation.

Wealth is awareness.

My mother taught me these things long before I understood their meaning.

She also taught me something else that shaped my entire life, my safety, my discernment, and my success.

The Right Side of My Brain – The Lesson That Saved My Life

When I was young, my mother made me study the right side of my brain, long before I even understood what that meant. She told me:

"If you understand your right brain, it will save your life."

I didn't know it then, but she was teaching me emotional intelligence, intuition, discernment, and self-trust. The right side of the brain is where intuition lives. It's where creativity flows. It's where your inner voice speaks. It's where you sense things before you can explain them.

My mother taught me how to:

Discern people's intentions.

Read energy before I read words.

Trust my instincts.

Create from my spirit.

Listen to God through intuition.

Move away from danger I couldn't yet describe.

Understand myself deeply.

Connect with others authentically.

Build ideas from vision instead of fear.

She wasn't teaching me science.

She was teaching me **survival**.

She was giving me the tools to navigate the world safely and successfully.

And she was right – it did save my life.

It saved me from friendships that meant me harm.

It saved me from environments I had no business being in.

It saved me from trusting people who were not aligned with my purpose.

It helped me build businesses.

It helped me read people clearly.

It helped me believe in myself.

It helped me trust my purpose even when my circumstances didn't match it.

My mother taught me that your intuition is your superpower.

Your creativity is your gift.

Your discernment is your protection.

Your emotional awareness is your wealth.

Everything I've created – businesses, brands, content, ideas, podcasts, impact – all came from the right side of my brain that my mother forced me to understand.

She didn't have much, but she gave me everything I needed.

Her Legacy Built My Millionaire Mindset

Today, I work hard because I saw her work even harder.

I build because she never had the chance to enjoy what she built.

I love people because she loved me deeply.

I encourage others because she encouraged me daily.

I uplift others because she uplifted me.

I walk in purpose because she placed purpose inside me.

Her affirmations shaped me.

Her warnings protected me.

Her sacrifices strengthened me.

Her wisdom elevated me.

Her spirit still guides me.

My mother is the reason I am who I am today.

And everything I teach in this book – investing, planning, mindset, credit, discipline, entrepreneurship, and building wealth comes from watching her create a life for us with so little.

She planted the millionaire mindset inside me long before I knew what to call it.

Her life taught me the importance of building wealth *while* you're here to enjoy it.

Her retirement taught me that tomorrow is not promised.

Her sacrifices taught me that love builds generational wealth.

And her legacy taught me that mindset is everything.

About The Author

Yvette Lloyd | Top-Ranked Podcast Host, Entrepreneur, and Empowerment Leader

Yvette Lloyd is a nationally recognized entrepreneur, award-winning podcast host, and highly respected community leader who has dedicated nearly two decades to building platforms that empower, educate, and inspire. As the creator and host of *Life Her Podcast*, Yvette has become a trusted voice in entrepreneurship, business growth, personal development, and faith-based leadership earning her podcast a ranking as one of the **Top 60 Black Entrepreneur Podcasts, currently ranked at #35** globally.

With 17 years as the owner of a successful daycare center, 5 years of podcasting, and 3 years as the owner of Life Her Podcast Studio, Yvette has transformed her personal journey of resilience into a powerful multimedia platform. Her work highlights the often untold stories of entrepreneurs, visionaries, and leaders while addressing real-life conversations around grief, healing, faith, and business.

Yvette's entrepreneurial footprint and impact have garnered widespread national media attention, including features in **Rolling Out, Beacon Journal, Voyage Ohio, Cleveland 19 News, Pretty Women Hustle, V&P Magazine, Bombshell by Bleu, Baltimore Times, Million Podcasts, Woman to Woman Talk, and others.** Her inspiring leadership and service to the community have been formally recognized with multiple awards and honors, including:

- **"Yvette Lloyd Day" December 20th, officially proclaimed by the City of Akron**

- **Congressional Recognition**

- **Summit County Council Commendation**

- Featured speaker at the inaugural **Women in Leadership Conference hosted by Congresswoman Emilia Sykes**

Through her FADIA Young Women's Program and her growing Life Her brand, Yvette has mentored countless young women and aspiring entrepreneurs, equipping them with the confidence, leadership skills, and practical tools to succeed professionally and personally.

Today, Yvette continues to expand her brand globally, blending entrepreneurship, media, community impact, and faith into a powerful movement that resonates across industries. She represents the modern blueprint of resilience, vision, and purpose-driven leadership.

Celebrity Guests Featured on *Life Her Podcast*

From your Voyage Ohio interview:

- **Iyanla Vanzant** (spiritual teacher & author)

- **Trina** (rapper Katrina Taylor)

- **Pilar Sanders** (Ex-wife of NFL legend Deion Sanders)

- **Pretty Vee** (comedian from *Wild 'N Out*)

- **Cora Jakes-Coleman** (motivational speaker & minister)

- **Kissie Lee** (actor & host)

- **Vina Love** (activist)

- **Sharaya J** (rapper & dancer)

- **Bridgett Pettis** (former WNBA coach/player)

- **Hot Boy Turk** & wife **Emani** (voyageohio.com, podbay.fm)

Recent High-Profile Guests (2024–2025)

- **Cori Broadus** – entrepreneur and daughter of hip-hop legend **Snoop Dogg**, who shared her life journey including health challenges and motherhood

- **Ragan Whiteside** – a Billboard-charting jazz flutist and award winner, discussing her music career and balancing family life

www.ingramcontent.com/pod-product-compliance
Lightning Source LLC
Chambersburg PA
CBHW051118200326
41518CB00016B/2551